HAL•LEONARD

VIOLIN

PLAY-ALONG

Lennon & McCartney

ISBN 978-1-61780-773-2

HAL•LEONARD® CORPORATION

7777 W. BLUEMOUND RD. P.O. BOX 13819 MILWAUKEE, WI 53213

Recorded and Produced by Jake Johnson
at Paradyme Productions
Violin by Jon C. Wagoner

Visit Hal Leonard Online at
www.halleonard.com

CONTENTS

All My Loving

Words and Music by John Lennon and Paul McCartney

1. Close your eyes ____ (3.) and I'll kiss ____ you, to-mor-row I'll miss ____
____ that I'm kiss - ing the lips I am miss -

____ you. Re - mem - ber ____ I'll al - ways ____ be true.
- ing, and hope that ____ my dreams will ____ come true.

And then while I'm a - way, ____ I'll write home ev - 'ry day, ____

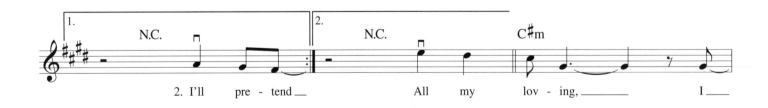

____ and I'll send all my lov - ing to you. ____

1.
2. I'll pre - tend ____

2.
All my lov - ing, ____ I ____

will send to you. _____ All _____ my

To Coda ⊕

lov - ing, _____ dar - ling, I'll _____ be true. _____

D.S. al Coda
(take 2nd ending)

Close your eyes _

⊕ **Coda**

All _____ my lov - ing, _____

all _____ my _____ lov - ing, ooh, _____ all _____ my _____

lov - ing, I will send _____ to _____ you. _____

And I Love Her

Words and Music by John Lennon and Paul McCartney

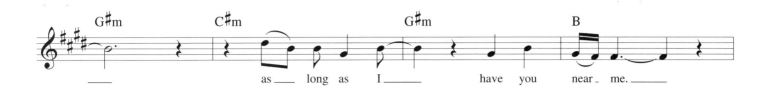

as _ long as I _____ have you near _ me. _____

Bright are the stars _____ that shine, _ dark is the sky. _____

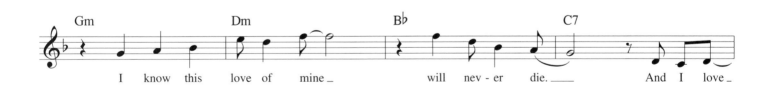

I know this love of mine _ will nev - er die. _____ And I love _

_ her. _____

Eleanor Rigby

Words and Music by John Lennon and Paul McCartney

I Saw Her Standing There

Words and Music by John Lennon and Paul McCartney

In My Life

Words and Music by John Lennon and Paul McCartney

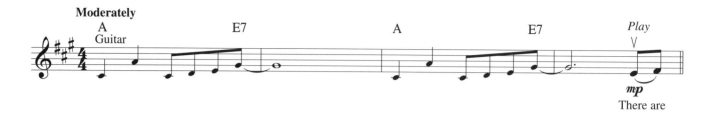

placeces I'll remember all my life, _____ though some have changed._ Some for-

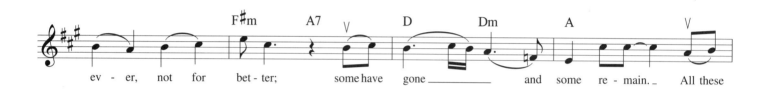

ever, not for better; some have gone _____ and some remain._ All these

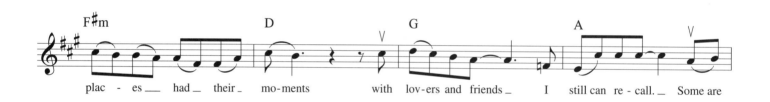

places __ had __ their _ moments with lov-ers and friends _ I still can re-call._ Some are

dead _ and _ some _ are _ liv-ing, in my _____ life I've loved them all. _

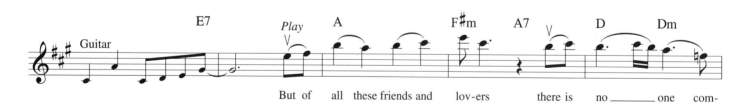

But of all these friends and lov-ers there is no _____ one com-

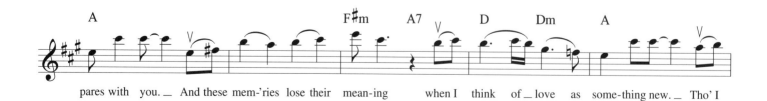

pares with you._ And these mem-'ries lose their mean-ing when I think of _ love as some-thing new._ Tho' I

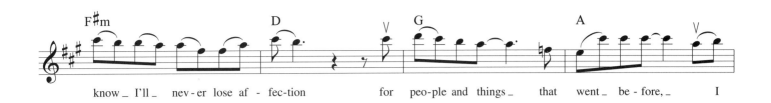

know __ I'll __ nev-er lose af - fec-tion   for peo-ple and things __ that went __ be - fore, __   I

know I'll of - ten stop and think a - bout them,   in my _____ life I love you more. __

Tho' I

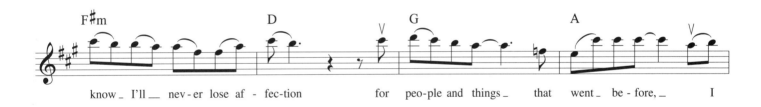

know __ I'll __ nev-er lose af - fec-tion   for peo-ple and things __ that went __ be - fore, __   I

know I'll of - ten stop and think a - bout them,   in my _____ life I love you more. __

In my _____ life I

love you more.

Michelle

Words and Music by John Lennon and Paul McCartney

Yellow Submarine

Words and Music by John Lennon and Paul McCartney

A Day in the Life

Words and Music by John Lennon and Paul McCartney

HAL•LEONARD INSTRUMENTAL PLAY-ALONG

Your favorite songs are arranged just for solo instrumentalists with this outstanding series. Each book includes a great full-accompaniment play-along CD so you can sound just like a pro! Check out **www.halleonard.com** to see all the titles available.

Disney Greats
Arabian Nights • Hawaiian Roller Coaster Ride • It's a Small World • Look Through My Eyes • Yo Ho (A Pirate's Life for Me) • and more.

_____	00841934	Flute	$12.95
_____	00841935	Clarinet	$12.95
_____	00841936	Alto Sax	$12.95
_____	00841937	Tenor Sax	$12.95
_____	00841938	Trumpet	$12.95
_____	00841939	Horn	$12.95
_____	00841940	Trombone	$12.95
_____	00841941	Violin	$12.95
_____	00841942	Viola	$12.95
_____	00841943	Cello	$12.95
_____	00842078	Oboe	$12.95

Glee
And I Am Telling You I'm Not Going • Defying Gravity • Don't Stop Believin' • Keep Holding On • Lean on Me • No Air • Sweet Caroline • True Colors • and more.

_____	00842479	Flute	$12.99
_____	00842480	Clarinet	$12.99
_____	00842481	Alto Sax	$12.99
_____	00842482	Tenor Sax	$12.99
_____	00842483	Trumpet	$12.99
_____	00842484	Horn	$12.99
_____	00842485	Trombone	$12.99
_____	00842486	Violin	$12.99
_____	00842487	Viola	$12.99
_____	00842488	Cello	$12.99

Movie Music
And All That Jazz • Come What May • I Am a Man of Constant Sorrow • I Walk the Line • Seasons of Love • Theme from Spider Man • and more.

_____	00842089	Flute	$10.95
_____	00842090	Clarinet	$10.95
_____	00842091	Alto Sax	$10.95
_____	00842092	Tenor Sax	$10.95
_____	00842093	Trumpet	$10.95
_____	00842094	Horn	$10.95
_____	00842095	Trombone	$10.95
_____	00842096	Violin	$10.95
_____	00842097	Viola	$10.95
_____	00842098	Cello	$10.95

Elvis Presley
All Shook Up • Blue Suede Shoes • Can't Help Falling in Love • Don't Be Cruel • Hound Dog • Jailhouse Rock • Love Me Tender • Return to Sender • and more.

_____	00842363	Flute	$12.99
_____	00842367	Trumpet	$12.99
_____	00842368	Horn	$12.99
_____	00842369	Trombone	$12.99
_____	00842370	Violin	$12.99
_____	00842371	Viola	$12.99
_____	00842372	Cello	$12.99

Sports Rock
Another One Bites the Dust • Centerfold • Crazy Train • Get Down Tonight • Let's Get It Started • Shout • The Way You Move • and more.

_____	00842326	Flute	$12.99
_____	00842327	Clarinet	$12.99
_____	00842328	Alto Sax	$12.99
_____	00842329	Tenor Sax	$12.99
_____	00842330	Trumpet	$12.99
_____	00842331	Horn	$12.99
_____	00842332	Trombone	$12.99
_____	00842333	Violin	$12.99
_____	00842334	Viola	$12.99
_____	00842335	Cello	$12.99

TV Favorites
The Addams Family Theme • The Brady Bunch • Green Acres Theme • Happy Days • Johnny's Theme • Linus and Lucy • NFL on Fox Theme • Theme from the Simpsons • and more.

_____	00842079	Flute	$10.95
_____	00842080	Clarinet	$10.95
_____	00842081	Alto Sax	$10.95
_____	00842082	Tenor Sax	$10.95
_____	00842083	Trumpet	$10.95
_____	00842084	Horn	$10.95
_____	00842085	Trombone	$10.95
_____	00842086	Violin	$10.95
_____	00842087	Viola	$10.95
_____	00842088	Cello	$10.95

FOR MORE INFORMATION, SEE YOUR LOCAL MUSIC DEALER, OR WRITE TO:

HAL•LEONARD® CORPORATION
7777 W. BLUEMOUND RD. P.O. BOX 13819 MILWAUKEE, WI 53213

Twilight
Bella's Lullaby • Decode • Eyes on Fire • Full Moon • Go All the Way (Into the Twilight) • Leave Out All the Rest • Spotlight (Twilight Remix) • Supermassive Black Hole • Tremble for My Beloved.

_____	00842406	Flute	$12.99
_____	00842407	Clarinet	$12.99
_____	00842408	Alto Sax	$12.99
_____	00842409	Tenor Sax	$12.99
_____	00842410	Trumpet	$12.99
_____	00842411	Horn	$12.99
_____	00842412	Trombone	$12.99
_____	00842413	Violin	$12.99
_____	00842414	Viola	$12.99
_____	00842415	Cello	$12.99

Twilight – New Moon
Almost a Kiss • Dreamcatcher • Edward Leaves • I Need You • Memories of Edward • New Moon • Possibility • Roslyn • Satellite Heart • and more.

_____	00842458	Flute	$12.99
_____	00842459	Clarinet	$12.99
_____	00842460	Alto Sax	$12.99
_____	00842461	Tenor Sax	$12.99
_____	00842462	Trumpet	$12.99
_____	00842463	Horn	$12.99
_____	00842464	Trombone	$12.99
_____	00842465	Violin	$12.99
_____	00842466	Viola	$12.99
_____	00842467	Cello	$12.99

Wicked
As Long As You're Mine • Dancing Through Life • Defying Gravity • For Good • I'm Not That Girl • Popular • The Wizard and I • and more.

_____	00842236	Book/CD Pack	$11.95
_____	00842237	Book/CD Pack	$11.95
_____	00842238	Alto Saxophone	$11.95
_____	00842239	Tenor Saxophone	$11.95
_____	00842240	Trumpet	$11.95
_____	00842241	Horn	$11.95
_____	00842242	Trombone	$11.95
_____	00842243	Violin	$11.95
_____	00842244	Viola	$11.95
_____	00842245	Cello	$11.95